FORK IN THE ROAD

A PLAY IN ONE ACT

JUDITH LACHEL FERGEN

authorHOUSE

AuthorHouse™
1663 Liberty Drive
Bloomington, IN 47403
www.authorhouse.com
Phone: 833-262-8899

Published by AuthorHouse 01/20/2025

ISBN: 979-8-8230-4048-8 (sc)
ISBN: 979-8-8230-4047-1 (e)

Library of Congress Control Number: 2024926821

Print information available on the last page.

Any people depicted in stock imagery provided by Getty Images are models, and such images are being used for illustrative purposes only. Certain stock imagery © Getty Images.

This book is printed on acid-free paper.

CONTENTS

To humble Hank and the heart of the game

"When you come to a fork in the road, take it." - *Yogi Berra*

FORK in the ROAD was first produced at the Old Court House Art Center on the historic Woodstock Square, Woodstock, Illinois, for one weekend, August 20, 21 and 22, 2004. With the help from a grant from The Illinois Arts Council, a local theatre company, TownSquare Players developed The Phoenix Workshop. This new workshop gave fledgling director Tim Curtis a chance to produce a new play, and playwright Fergen, the opportunity to see her work come to life.

Cast

Hank. . . . . .Neil Arsenty

Molly. . . . . Sheri Shorter

Jake. . . . . .Jim Pierce

Maggie . . . . Bree Pavey

Renee. . . . . .Janaan Rose

Walter/ Cliff. . . . . .David Lindquist

Dean . . . . .Jason Bickham

Amy. . . . . .Julie Billimack

Yvonne . . . . Jenny Neathery

Youth. . . . . Haley Brooks Michling

Staff

Artistic Direction . . . . Timothy R. Curtis

Technical Direction . . . . Paul Bayer

Production . . . . Laurie Faith Gibson, Patricia Gonzales

Set Design . . . . Charles Rucker

Costumes and Props . . . . Our Cast and Staff

ACKNOWLEDGMENTS

This play is a collaboration of my muses, both living and gone. I owe a huge debt to Bob Riner of the Theatre Department at McHenry County College, Crystal Lake, Illinois. Bob was instrumental in helping me with a "play-in-progress", enabling me to hear my characters and receive audience feedback. Thank you to my readers for their participation and patience as I made my changes. Many thanks to my husband Larry, who spent countless hours in the beginning, typing and correcting. Thanks to Joe Dugo, who helped me with stats, you are the consummate fan! Thanks to Tim Curtis who believed in the story enough to be my extra pair of eyes and take it to the much needed level with his direction. Thank you to my daughter Chelsea, who, unwittingly helps me recognize that mothers were once daughters. And finally, thank you to my daughter Ravelle, who came up with the ending solution. Without her idea, there would be no beginning.

Reference: <u>Hank Aaron - Baseball Legends</u> by James Tackach

© 1992 - Chelsea House Publishers pp. 10-13

Reference: "You Got It" by Roy Orbison

© 1989 – Mystery Girl Album – Virgin Records Atlantic

FORK IN THE ROAD - CHARACTER LIST:

HANK AARON VINETTE, 24 - veterinary student

WALTER VINETTE, 35 - HANK'S father

RENEE VINETTE, 35 - HANK'S mother

JAKE, late 20's - owner of diner

MOLLY, 21 - JAKE'S sister

MAGGIE, late 20's - waitress

DEAN, 23 - MAGGIE'S brother

CLIFF, 35 - truck driver

AMY, 25 - patron

YVONNE, 30 - patron and AMY'S sister

YOUTH at telephone, 18

FEMALE TRAVELER, 30

Note: minor characters could double up

<u>TIME</u>

Spring 1998

<u>PLACE</u>

Hank's prologue begins before the first act. Curtain opens on the inside of the Fork in the Road diner, which is located in rural Illinois, approximately one hour east of the Iowa border. The diner's interior design is circa 1960's. Stage right has a short counter on an angle with three padded stools and a cash register at the far end. A sign above the counter reads: Try Our World Famous Flippins! The kitchen is out of sight off stage right. The main entrance door is mid-center, with a pay phone between the door and two or more padded booths that look out a window. An old juke box backs up to stage left. Next to it, down stage, an opening with restroom sign above it. Unseen living quarters upstairs over the diner are accessed off stage left.

HANK'S PROLOGUE

(HANK enters down stage left with spotlight, stops at proscenium and addresses audience)

HANK

When I was eight years old, the only thing that my buddies and I could think about, was getting outside to play baseball! As soon as the good weather came 'round in the spring, we'd daydream at our school desks, gazing out the windows until recess. Or better yet, counting the minutes until they'd let us loose and we could grab our gear to play.... And if we weren't playing baseball, we were talking baseball and trading baseball cards! You remember that gum that came in the packs of cards, don't ya? Mostly the gum was all dry and brittle with that white powder on it, but nobody cared. You'd rip open the package and shove the gum into your mouth as you'd look at your treasures. Maybe you'd be real lucky and get a card you didn't have. That really takes me back,.... Topps baseball cards.... If you were a New York Yankees fan, you would trade anything for a Dave Winfield or Reggie Jackson. My buddies and I followed the Chicago teams. I would find a Ryne Sandberg, a Fergie Jenkins, or even a Ron Santo card in my lunch bag, while other kids **just** got homemade treats.

(Lights up on couple seated at a baseball game, mid-center)

HANK (Cont'd)

There they are - Renee and Walter Vinette. My parents - the baseball nuts! Actually, there <u>we</u> were in Atlanta. It's April 8th, 1974 and Mom was pregnant with me at the time. For vacations, we'd travel to other ball parks. It was a challenge, too, because Dad followed the American League teams, and Mom, the National league. Their love for the game of baseball was so great that it would postpone, or in some cases, stop arguments completely. It's no wonder that I thought the song, "Take Me Out to the Ballgame" was a lullaby!.... Some men hold a baseball in their hand and try to recognize players' signatures from the past. Some hold an old baseball glove up to their face to block the sunshine and smell the worn leather as a journey back to boyhood. For me,... I just think of my folks. How lucky could a kid get?

(HANK gestures towards couple, his spotlight out)

RENEE

You know Wally, this baby will be here soon and we still haven't agreed on a name.

WALTER

Walter Junior is fine with me. You're the fussy one.

RENEE

You're **so** positive that we're having a boy! Fine, what if we name the baby after the next guy who hits a homer?

WALTER

Deal...I'm hoping to witness a little baseball history.

RENEE

Me too! Hank's up, and he's due. .... I gotta hear the play by play on my radio.

(RENEE puts in her ear phone and turns on her transistor radio)

RADIO ANNOUNCER

Another standing ovation for Henry Aaron. He's up to bat for the second time. Aaron walked in the second inning. Hammerin' Hank is on his way to the plate as the umpire hands over another infrared coded ball. If number "44" connects - somebody's gonna have a fine souvenir....Okay - Al Downing winds up,... misses in the dirt. Ball one. The crowd's booing. Dusty Baker is on deck, no doubt, watching to see if Babe Ruth's home run record will be beaten here at home.... The catcher signals. Downing delivers. **THERE IT GOES!!!** Hank Aaron has just broken Babe Ruth's record for homer 715! The only thing Dodger Bill Buckner could do at the fence, was to wave it good-bye! Listen to that crowd! Hank's family is climbing out of their box seats to congratulate him!

(RENEE turns off the radio, she and WALTER shout over the crowd)

WALTER

That's it! Baby Hank it's going to be! Hank Aaron Vinette. I like the sound of that.

RENEE

But, what if it's a girl?

WALTER

Uh,...a girl,...well, I guess Henrietta could work.

RENEE

HENRIETTA?.... We'll see about that!

(Lights down on couple, spotlight up on HANK))

HANK

You see.....I had to make this trip!

(HANK exits stage left, curtain closes Blackout)

ACT I, SCENE 1

(Early evening, late spring 1998. Curtain opens as JAKE, the owner of the Fork in the Road Diner is seated at back booth, going over the days receipts. Two women are seated at the counter)

JAKE

Molly!... Molly, get in here, damn it!

(MOLLY enters stage right from kitchen, places boxes on counter)

MOLLY

What, Jake?

JAKE

Did you pay for the produce out of the till again?

MOLLY

Yeah,...you weren't here and the new safe was locked.

JAKE

I can't believe it! You can't remember a simple lock combination?

MOLLY

Well, I wrote it down on one of my order pads, but....

JAKE

Can't trust you with anything! You forgot to get a receipt from him.

MOLLY

No, Tony gave me one. It's in there!

1

JAKE

No it ain't! I went over the stack of bills twice! We're short 28 dollars and change and unless you can come with the receipt, it's coming outta your pocket!

(MOLLY reaches in a pocket and pulls out the receipt, crosses to JAKE and lays it on the table)

MOLLY

Here, I knew he gave me one.

JAKE

When are you gonna wise up? The guy's married!

MOLLY

Tony's divorce will be final next month. He said so this morning.

JAKE

Yeah, right after he turns into Prince Charming and trades his beater truck in for a white horse! You sure can pick 'em, Molly.

MOLLY

Well, I believe him.

JAKE

I suppose you were so busy making goo-goo eyes at Tony that you weren't paying attention to what the HELL you were doing.

MOLLY

Just stop about Tony. Where'd you go earlier, anyway?

JAKE

None of your business. Besides, you wouldn't have had any problem with the safe if you weren't so scatter-brained!

(MOLLY returns to counter, muttering)

MOLLY

Rather be scatter-brained than crude.

JAKE

What was that?

MOLLY

I said, ...I think I'll fix some food.

JAKE

Hey! I'm still short 75 cents.

MOLLY

The pay phone at the interstate gas station is out of order again. A kid borrowed some change to call home.

JAKE

Borrowed? Heh! You ain't never gonna see him again. Pay up!

MOLLY

FINE!!! HERE CHEAPSKATE!

JAKE

How in the hell am I supposed to balance out the register if you give in to every charity case that comes in here?

(JAKE rises and begins gathering up receipts, MOLLY continues to work behind counter muttering)

JAKE (Cont'd)

What did you say?

MOLLY

Never mind!!

JAKE

"Never mind" is right! And don't you call me a cheapskate again! You're forgettin' that you live upstairs for nothin' you ungrateful …. miserable female, etc., etc.

(Jake exits to kitchen as counter customer gets MOLLY's attention)

AMY

Excuse me, miss. Did I overhear you saying that Tony's Produce stops here?

MOLLY

Yes, why? Do you know Tony?

YVONNE

Do we know Tony? Stand up, Amy.

(AMY gets up from the counter and is obviously pregnant)

YVONNE (Cont'd)

Amy knows Tony, … I would say she knows him intimately. What do you think?

MOLLY

Are you Mrs. Portofino?

YVONNE

In person!

AMY

Stop it, Yvonne! I can speak for myself.... Yes. I'm Tony's wife.

MOLLY

But,... I don't understand.... Tony said ... um, you are supposed to get....

AMY

Look, you can see for yourself that I'm almost 6 months along. I don't know what line of bull he's been feeding you, but Tony's not going anywhere with you!

MOLLY

But, he said ....

YVONNE

You stupid girl! I'll bet you think you're the only one.

MOLLY

What do you mean?

YVONNE

I've seen Tony's truck parked for hours at another diner, in the next county. If it makes any difference to you, the waitress there is knocked up by him too. My sister and I thought we should take a little ride to fill you girls in.

MOLLY

There must be some mistake!

AMY

Yeah - the mistake's name is Tony!

YVONNE

Say, ... you're not pregnant, too, are you?

MOLLY

No, I'm not!

AMY

Come on, Yvonne. I've had enough!....Oh,... by the way,

(AMY picks up tomato from crate and hands it to MOLLY)

... you better tell your boss to shop for his vegetables someplace else.

(AMY and YVONNE turn to exit, leaving MOLLY speechless. JAKE enters from kitchen)

JAKE

Good work, Molly. Now I gotta look for another produce delivery guy!

MOLLY

Jake, you don't understand!

JAKE

What's to understand? Tony's populating the state, one waitress at a time. I heard the whole thing from the kitchen.

MOLLY

Go ahead, ... tell me "I told you so", then let me be!

JAKE

Yeah, you sure can pick 'em. You're never gonna replace Dean, but you could move up a little higher on the food chain.

(JAKE exits to kitchen. MOLLY picks up a tomato and throws it at the wall just as HANK comes through the door with a thermos)

HANK

Whoa!

MOLLY

(MOLLY turns around startled)

OH!.... C-c- can I help you?

HANK

I just need quarters for the phone.

MOLLY

Sure....

(checks register)

Oh,...sorry, we're out of quarters. I need to ask Jake for some.

(a youth enters to use the phone)

HANK

Did you know the phone at the gas station off the interstate is on the fritz? They sent me down here.

MOLLY

Yes, we've had a steady stream of people using ours all day. Wait,...Silly me,...I have tip change!

(MOLLY reaches in her pockets for coins and hands HANK coins for bills)

7

MOLLY (Cont'd)

Here.

HANK

Thanks.

(HANK turns to go to phone, but it is being used, then sits at counter)

HANK (Cont'd)

Miss, could I get a cup of coffee, please?

(MOLLY serves him as JAKE enters from kitchen)

MOLLY

Jake, I'm out of quarters and dimes.

(JAKE exits. Caller using phone exits while a woman comes in and begs to use the phone before HANK just as he reaches it)

TRAVELER

Excuse me - It's an emergency! My car .... quit down the road....

(HANK steps back)

TRAVELER (Cont'd)

Thank you, sir....Thank you.

(HANK returns to counter)

MOLLY

Need a warmer?

HANK

No, thanks.

(Traveler leaves, as HANK rises to use the phone, it rings and first caller comes back in to answer it. Frustrated, HANK slumps into the nearest booth. JAKE enters, goes to register to refill coins. He notices that HANK is now at a booth instead of at the counter)

JAKE

Hey! Hey you! What do you think this is - musical chairs?? Make up your mind where you're gonna sit so the girl don't have to run around and clean up after you, huh? Geez!

(JAKE closes the register and turns to see the tomato mess)

JAKE (Cont'd)

What the,... Molly!

MOLLY

I'll clean it up!

(JAKE returns to kitchen, MOLLY starts cleaning up wall)

HANK

That's quite a fastball you have. Felt good, didn't it.

MOLLY

It sure did! I don't know what came over me.

HANK

Well, it looks like no harm was done.

MOLLY

Not to the wall, anyway. Would you like anything else?

HANK

No, thanks, Molly.

MOLLY

Hey,...do I know you?

HANK

Well, I'm Hank. And, uh... "Molly" is written on your blouse.

MOLLY

Oh yeah....Nice to meet you. Where're you from?

HANK

Nodaway, Iowa.

MOLLY

Nodaway,... nope, never heard of it.

HANK

I'm not surprised. It's a real small town west of Des Moines.

MOLLY

Oh,... what brings you this way?

HANK

I'm headed to Chicago,... to do a favor for my mom.

MOLLY

You want some coffee for the road?

(pointing to HANK'S thermos)

HANK

Umm,...no.

MOLLY

How 'bout tea?

(MOLLY places coffee pot on table)

HANK

Uh....

MOLLY

We've got a new herbal kind.

HANK

No, ...I...

MOLLY

Really,... it's no trouble to boil some water.

HANK

No,... no tea.

MOLLY

Well, we're out of hot chocolate. Why don't I rinse this out and fill it with juice.

(MOLLY tries to take thermos from HANK)

HANK

No, I can't open it....

MOLLY

I could run the cap under warm water to loosen it up. Here,....

(MOLLY takes thermos)

HANK

No! Don't! Mom's in there!

MOLLY

Oh, my God!

(MOLLY juggles thermos, HANK takes it)

HANK

I'm sorry!.... I didn't know how else to say it.

(MOLLY grabs coffee from table, and downs most of it, all the time   staring at the thermos. Telephone caller exits.)

MOLLY

Your mom's ashes are in there? Don't ashes usually get put in one of those jars ?

(JAKE enters from kitchen - has "business" at counter)

HANK

Yes....an urn, but it wasn't practical for my plans.

MOLLY

What kind of plans? Traveling across the country scaring waitresses?

HANK

No. Look,... I said, "I'm sorry". I'll use the phone, then leave.

(HANK gets up)

MOLLY

No, wait....I'm okay now. Really,... here, sit down and have some coffee.
I drank your cup. Only,... could you, uh, put the thermos on the seat?

(HANK sits back down, puts thermos on chair, MOLLY pours
coffee)

HANK

Are you sure I'm not keeping you from anything?

(HANK gets nasty look from JAKE who exits to kitchen)

MOLLY

No, I could use a break.

HANK

After shocking you like that, I owe you an explanation.

MOLLY

Oh, it wasn't only you. This was the afternoon from HELL before you
walked in.

HANK

Well, as I was saying,... The favor is actually her final wish. I'm on my way
to Chicago with my mom's ashes. Since she enjoyed baseball so much, she
wanted to have them sprinkled on her favorite ballpark, Wrigley Field.

MOLLY

Did she pass away recently?

HANK

It was about three and a half years ago.

MOLLY

How come you waited 'til now to go?

HANK

Um,... well, I just...

MOLLY

Sorry. That's none of my business.

HANK

That's okay.... I <u>just</u> found out about her request after Easter.

MOLLY

Oh.

HANK

Yeah, Dad told me when he was hospitalized after a stroke. He was upset and ashamed to admit that he waited too long to deal with it. We could have gone together.

MOLLY

Is he still,...I mean,...is he at home?

HANK

He's at a nursing home. He's pretty much bed-ridden.

MOLLY

Any brothers or sisters?

HANK

Nope - just me and South Paw.

MOLLY

South Paw? Is that your grandpa?

HANK

No. He just <u>thinks</u> he is - South Paw is my dad's dog.

MOLLY

Oh, I see.... Anyway, so why use a thermos?

HANK

That was Mr. Ebbets' idea. He's a groundskeeper at the ball park and an old friend of my boss's family.

MOLLY

I get it. Easier to smuggle the ashes in that way.....

(HANK looks at his watch)

HANK

It's after 6 o'clock already? I need to make a call. Excuse me.

(HANK goes to use phone as MOLLY takes coffee pot to counter, then exits to kitchen)

HANK

Hello. Bob Ebbets, please.

BOB

Yeah, this is...

HANK

Hi, Mr. Ebbets. It's Hank Vinette. I work with Doc Gooden. We spoke a couple of weeks ago about...

BOB

Oh, yeah, yeah. I remember. You're the kid with the ashes.

HANK

Right. So, where should I meet you tomorrow?

BOB

Uh,... well,... where are you now?

HANK

I'm just off the interstate. Why?

BOB

The Iowa side?

HANK

No, the Illinois side, closer to Rock Falls.

BOB

Well, ummmm,...I been havin' second thoughts.

HANK

What? We must have a bad connection. Did you say....

BOB

I was, uh, thinkin that, uh, maybe this ain't such a great idea, after all. You don't want me to get canned, do ya?

HANK

No, of course not, but,...I drove all...

BOB

You callin' from your car?

HANK

No, from a pay phone,... I don't have a car phone.

BOB

You should get one of them. They're pretty handy.

HANK

That's besides the point!

BOB

Now hold on there. I called you yesterday, but there was nobody home. Don't you have an answering machine, either?

HANK

No. You could have tried Doc's office!

BOB

I did. I left a message on his machine last night!

HANK

Great! That does me alot of good now!... Wait! What about during batting practice, or...,...a ballpark tour?

BOB

Listen, security is more uptight than ever. It ain't happenin'. Go home, kid, and wait 'til next year. Tell Doc I said "Hi". Sorry.

(MOLLY enters from kitchen)

HANK

You're sorry? That's it? YOU'RE SORRY? **IDIOT!**

(he slams phone down and slumps back into the booth)

17

Damn! Son of a ...

(MOLLY clears her throat)

MOLLY

Uhmmm....

HANK

What?

MOLLY

Are you okay?

HANK

NO! I'm not okay!

(he picks up a metal napkin holder and pushes the empty side flap, making an annoying sound)

MOLLY

Well, if you want to throw something, I have more tomatoes in the kitchen.

HANK

I would need at least a bushel! Ebbets bailed out on me!

MOLLY

Oh, that's too bad!

HANK

Got scared he'd get caught and fired. I thought he had it all figured out....

MOLLY

Maybe, someday they'll change the law.

HANK

Not a chance 'cause every baseball fan would have their ashes spread on their favorite ball park....The pitcher's mound would be as high as the upper deck!...

MOLLY

Is it weird for you handling your mom's ashes?

HANK

Well, when I was spooning the ashes into the thermos, I tried to imagine her watching me and how comical she'd think it was.... At first, after she died,... I'd find myself talking out loud to the container. Sometimes I'd update her about the box scores...You must think that sounds crazy.

MOLLY

No,... not really.... But didn't your mom tell you about her wish before she died?

HANK

She mentioned it jokingly when I was in high school, but I never took it seriously.

MOLLY

I think you're pretty brave.... I mean, it's hard enough to say goodbye, but to do it more than once,....

HANK

I was <u>so angry</u> that she died with out any warning. Just like that, she was gone.

MOLLY

<u>How</u> did it happen?

HANK

It was a brain aneurysm. We were on our way back home after spending Dad's birthday weekend in Milwaukee. He wanted to see the Brewers play the White Sox. Mom complained of a headache, so she laid down in the back seat to try to get rid of it. The last thing she said to us was, "The ballpark food was great, but the pitching stunk!"

MOLLY

Wow....

HANK

Yeah,....so,...here I am. The plan was <u>so good</u>. Damn Ebbets!

MOLLY

What a shame! There must be some other way.

HANK

This **was** the other way! My original plan was to smuggle the ashes in two plastic, air-tight bags - in my jacket pockets. I imagined just the right moment would come while the crowd was cheering for a homerun, when I could lean over the bleachers wall and empty out the bags.

MOLLY

Well, that sounds like a great idea! Why can't you still go ahead and do that?

HANK

Somebody beat me to it!

MOLLY

I don't understand.

HANK

A guy brought his dad's ashes to the ballpark, just like I was going to do - in plastic bags in his pockets. Just as he started to let the ashes loose during the seventh inning stretch, the wind picked up and blew them back into the faces of a nasty bunch of bleacher bums.

MOLLY

Oh, that's awful!

HANK

It got worse....The crowd around him figured out what he was doing and **just** what had blown all over them. People were shaking off his dad's ashes from their hair and clothes, not to mention their eyes, and they started yelling for the security guards! Before he knew it, he was being hauled away, while what little ashes left were getting soaked up by the spilled beer.

MOLLY

The poor guy!

HANK

Yeah,.... well,.... After that, they really beefed up security at the park. I heard the whole story from my boss when I told him about my plan. That's when he made the call to his friend, about the groundskeeper.... He's all right, Doc Gooden.

MOLLY

Are you a doctor?

HANK

Not yet. I'm studying to be a veterinarian. I just started an internship in a small practice, so it was really pushing it to ask for any time off.... Right now, Doc's covering for me. He was even good enough to keep South Paw, too....Wait 'til I tell him that Ebbets got cold feet!... Even if this whole plan had to be postponed, before I'd get the chance to come back, baseball season would be over and Wrigley Field will be closed.

MOLLY

Gee, Hank,... it's too bad that you have to go back home after you've come this far.

HANK

HOME? NO!

MOLLY

But, I thought you just said...

HANK

I can't turn around now! I promised my dad that I would take care of this. There's nobody else. I can't possibly face him before I do!

MOLLY

But how?

HANK

I don't know.... It's as if I'm standing at the foot of the Big Green Monster without a bat or ball.

MOLLY

A monster?

HANK

The Big Green Monster is a huge wall at Fenway Park in Boston. A batter has to hit a towering home run to make it over the wall. It's some sight to see. There's got to be a way to get over this wall - a rope,... or a trampoline,..

MOLLY

... or a helicopter.

HANK

<u>Now</u> you're talkin'!

MOLLY

Seriously,...

HANK

I tell ya, Molly,... my mom would probably like the helicopter idea! As for me, lately I've dealt with so many things I never counted on. Nothing sounds out of the question.

MOLLY

I remember going through all my folks stuff after they were gone. You're right, it's alot of emotions and work all at once. I didn't know what to save or what to give away. You should have seen the stack of boxes I had for the Salvation Army!

HANK

When did they pass away?

MOLLY

Oh, they're not dead. They went to Las Vegas for a second honeymoon and decided to stay there. That was eight years ago.

HANK

What about the holidays?

MOLLY

The first couple of years they'd visit at Christmas. My mom didn't drive and Dad hated having to do it all. There's no airport close to here, so they haven't been back .

HANK

And that was it?

MOLLY

Well, three years ago Dad had surgery and I went to stay with them. We were such strangers…They wouldn't let me help with anything, so a few days later I came home.

HANK

That's rough.

MOLLY

I guess some trips just aren't meant to be.

HANK

Maybe…but I'm going to Chicago tomorrow. There's a 1:20 game and Mom and I are going to be there!….You see, I'm so screwed up about this whole thing. Only Ebbets and my boss knew, and now you. You're a great listener, Molly,… and me, I'm just running on and on… I'm sure you have work to do.

MOLLY

Work can wait. This is much more interesting than hearing the regulars complaining about road work or the weather. I want to hear more about your mom. She must have been some baseball nut!

HANK

She was. Every spring, for as long as I can remember, she'd talk about the first game her dad took her to see at Wrigley Field. She was instantly in love with the ivy on the outfield walls and the view of Lake Michigan over the roof tops. Her face would light up when she'd describe the smells of the ball park, the crazy fans, and the excitement of the triple play she saw! Do you like baseball?

MOLLY

I'm not sure. I've only been to one game, and that was back in high school.

My boyfriend brought me to see his cousin in a Little League, but because the port-o-potty line was so long, I missed the only hit he got. I do remember the families and friends that were completely engrossed in the game tho, and just being outside on a summer day with Dean, was better than being cooped up in school or at the diner.

HANK

Really? One Little League game? I was raised on it.

(HANK notices that MOLLY'S attention is elsewhere)

HANK (Cont'd)

Molly,... what is it?

MOLLY

Oh,... nothing. Sorry...Was your dad as crazy about baseball as your mom?

HANK

Oh yeah,... but he was from Detroit.

MOLLY

So, what's wrong with that?

HANK

Just that Mom followed the National League and the Detroit Tigers are in the American League.

MOLLY

So, did they get into arguments about their teams?

HANK

Well, they would call it "Discussing the Game" They would take turns listening to the radio and watching the TV, depending on which game was being televised. Looking back, I think they really made an effort to respect each other's favorite teams. They were baseball nuts all right.... They even named me after the famous player, Hank Aaron.... Some families went to Disneyland or the Grand Canyon on their vacations. Mom would send away to different ballparks for their schedules so we could plan our trips around certain games.

MOLLY

So, does your dad want his ashes on the Detroit park?

HANK

No, but he has insisted on being buried all decked out in a Detroit Tigers uniform - Baseball cap and all!

(Hank and Molly laugh)

.... Right now, I hate to even think about that.

JAKE

Hey, Molly!

(He doesn't wait for her to answer and shouts again)

Molly!

MOLLY

What?

JAKE

Go turn on the outside sign.

MOLLY

But it's not dark yet!

JAKE

Just do it now! It might bring in more supper traffic.

MOLLY

Okay, okay! You know, Jake, it wouldn't kill you to say "please" once in a while!

JAKE

FINE! Please, Molly dear, would you please turn on the God damn sign!

(MOLLY gets up, flips switches and returns to booth)

HANK

Is that your husband?

MOLLY

No, I'm not married! Jake's my brother!

HANK

Your brother! Is he always so pleasant?

MOLLY

Yeah - As you can see, he works at it.

(They both look over towards the counter to make sure JAKE isn't there, then laugh)

(Stage lights down on HANK and MOLLY as JAKE enters from kitchen to counter and addresses audience)

JAKE

My parents,...what a couple of cowards.... I remember the phone call like it was yesterday.

(phone rings, JAKE answers)

Fork in the Road.

DAD (voice only)

Jake, my boy! The weather's great here in Vegas! Guess who you're talkin' to? Why the biggest high-roller west of the Mississippi, that's who! I took the casino for a hellava ride last night, so we're cruisin' around here for one of them there condos! I was thinkin',...you don't need to go off to that "Q-lernary" school! You're a great cook already! I know 'cause I taught ya myself. Besides, you're old enough to take care of the diner. I'll have some papers drawn up and mail them. Shoulda done this years ago! I'd put your mom on, but she's in the gift shop. Say "Hi" to Molly. Talk to ya later. Bye!

(JAKE slams phone down)

JAKE

DAMN HIM! He never even let me get a word in edgewise.... Just <u>where</u> did they get the idea that I wanted this out-in-the-middle-of-nowhere-diner? What about learning to become a <u>real</u> chef? What about preparing something more interesting than eggs over-easy, with a side of bacon and white toast?... On top of that, I got my kid sister to watch. Do you have any idea what it's like to keep an eye on a teen-age girl? Between the mood swings and boys comin' around,... Geez! Where do ya go to school for that?...Sometimes I think about unloading this place for whatever I could get for it.... Splitting 50/50 with Molly... don't know....

(JAKE exits stage right. Stage lights back up on HANK and MOLLY)

HANK

Excuse me,...all this coffee is well, ...

(HANK rises)

MOLLY

Oh, sure- the men's room is over there.

(HANK exits as a woman enters through the center door)

MAGGIE

Hi there, Molly!

MOLLY

Hi, Magpie! I thought you were out of town with Neil.

MAGGIE

That makes two of us. He took off with his buddies to go fishin'. I guess my "lures" aren't what they used to be! Who was that at the booth with you,...a new vendor?

MOLLY

No, you've worked here long enough to know that vendors only stop in the mornings.

(She gazes towards the men's room)

MAGGIE

Well, he's not dressed like an insurance salesman.

MOLLY

No, he's just a nice guy passing through.

MAGGIE

You haven't sat down in a booth with anybody but Tony for months. What gives?

MOLLY

Nothing! And don't you dare mention Tony's name to me again!

MAGGIE

You two on the outs?

MOLLY

His wife was here this morning.

MAGGIE

Damn! All the juicy stuff always happens when I'm not here. Was there a cat fight?

MOLLY

It was a nightmare! She and her sister heard Jake and me talking about Tony. Before I knew it, they were all over me about how stupid I am to believe anything he says 'cause his wife's pregnant.

MAGGIE

NO!

MOLLY

They also said that a waitress along one of his stops is expecting too!

MAGGIE

Oh, honey....

MOLLY

I'm such a fool. Just today he told me that his divorce was a few weeks away!

MAGGIE

The bastard! You're well rid of him.

MOLLY

I hope it's not busy tonight. I'd just like this day to be over.

(HANK opens the men's room door and the girls both look at him. Embarrassed at the attention, HANK looks himself over quickly)

HANK

What?....Do I have toilet paper on my shoe, or worse?

MOLLY

What could be worse?

(MAGGIE whispers to her and gestures below her waist as if to a zipper)

MOLLY (Cont'd)

Oh! Uh, ... no, nothing's wrong!!

(MOLLY goes to the counter to avoid anymore embarrassment)

MAGGIE

Molly - won't you introduce me?

MOLLY

This is Hank, uh...

HANK

Hank Aaron . Pleased to meet you, Magpie.

(MAGGIE glares at MOLLY)

MAGGIE

It's really Maggie, but my friends gave me that nickname. Hey,...wasn't Hank Aaron a famous base,....

(HANK interrupts her mid-sentence and looks secretly at MOLLY)

HANK

You're right. I'm no relation, just named after him.

MAGGIE

You're a baseball player then, from a local farm team?

MOLLY

No, he's a veterinarian. Gosh, Magpie, you're so nosy!!

MAGGIE

I'm just being friendly.

MOLLY

Well, "Miss Friendly", I need to go upstairs and change my shoes. Could you be a pal and watch the place a minute?

MAGGIE

Sure, I got it covered.

MOLLY

Thanks.

(MOLLY exits. MAGGIE starts chatting non-stop)

MAGGIE

I'm worried about her. All she ever does is work, work, work. Sweet kid, too. You see, her folks ran off to Vegas, like a couple of degenerates and left her here with Jake to run this place. That was pretty hard on her. She was only 15 years at the time! I sort of took her under my wing. She was a lost puppy for the longest time...But the biggest shock came when my younger brother Dean died.....

HANK

I'm sorry....

MAGGIE (Cont'd)

Thank you .... Dean and Molly were thick as thieves since high school,... practically inseparable. If you saw Molly, Dean wasn't far behind and vice-versa. I miss him so. Life is so unfair!

(Lights down on HANK and MOLLY. DEAN enters with leather jacket over one shoulder, from down stage left to proscenium and addresses audience)

DEAN

You got that right - Life is unfair! I make it through high school football without a single broken bone or a concussion. Then, I hang in there during combat in the Gulf War. I tried to write to Molly as often as I could to assure her that I was okay,... I know she was really worried about me. Thankfully, I make it home in one piece. I was lucky enough to get my old job back, too.... A few months later, I get a great deal on a buddy's motorcycle that he needed to sell.... Molly and I used to ride it for hours.

33

All right all you parents out there, I know what you're thinkin', but you're wrong! We wore our helmets! Never had an accident.,…not so much as a scratch! You know what takes me out? This is embarrassing - a garage door. I tell you, people - use your remote controls! I used to hit the automatic close switch and run out as the door was closing, just like Indiana Jones. One day I tripped, hit the concrete floor and broke my neck. How's that for FAIR?

(DEAN exits left, lights back up on MAGGIE and HANK)

HANK

Were they engaged?

MAGGIE

Yeah, except for the ring …. All she's got left is his jacket. For months after he was gone, Molly still read his horoscope out loud before hers and kept her eye on the parking lot looking for his truck. I wish she'd move in with me, just to get away from here!

(MOLLY enters from downstage left to proscenium, addresses audience)

MOLLY

When I was 8 years old, the only thing I wanted to do was to go outside. All summer long I had inside chores to do,… same with after school and on weekends. As soon as my chores were finished, I bolted for the back lot and my swing set. Once outside, I could be anyone,… not just Molly. Sometimes, I'd swing so high that I imagined I'd put myself into orbit and become an astronaut. Other times, I'd unhook the swing from the rusty top bar and hang upside-down. Maybe a traveling circus would see me and ask me to join them because they needed a trapeze artist…. Cold weather wouldn't stop me, either. I loved building snow forts. I'd add to the construction with empty barrels, brooms and a plank of wood for a draw bridge. One year, after a snow storm, Jake and I made a huge snow girl in the front of the diner. We made sure that she was eye-catching, with a big chest. We laughed so hard that I peed in my snowsuit. That was the last time I saw my brother bust a gut, laughing like that! It took most of that morning with all the regulars winking at Jake, for my mom to go out and see what we had built. Of course, she was embarrassed and made Dad go knock down our hard work. The first Christmas without our parents, I wanted to have a party here with Maggie and some of the customers. They were all like one big, noisy, happy family to me. Maggie liked the idea, but not Jake. He said that he had to put up with us all day and the last thing he wanted to do after hours was to put on the feed bag with us! I was so mad that I made a thermos of hot chocolate, got all bundled up and spent early Christmas Eve sitting on the swing set, being an astronomer with an empty paper towel roll. Maggie and her brother, Dean came to rescue me....They forced me to come inside, where it was warm and taught me to play a card game called Crazy Eights. It was, what I call " a worst-best day". The holiday was depressing, but I fell in love with Dean.

(lights down on MOLLY, back up on HANK and MAGGIE)

HANK

Why does she stay? I mean, her brother treats her like dirt.

MAGGIE

Jake's all noise. He'd never hit her or anything. But, on the other hand, he doesn't exactly give her any encouragement. This place is all Molly knows. Between you and me, I think she dreams about her parents coming back....I'm sorry,...I don't know why I'm going on so.

HANK

Just that kinda' day.

MAGGIE

Molly gets upset when I bring up my movin' idea – so mum's the word – okay?

HANK

Sure.

(MOLLY returns to booth)

MOLLY

Can I get you two anything?

MAGGIE

Nope,

HANK

No thanks, ... but I do have one question.

(MAGGIE thinks he's going to ask something regarding her revelation, so she gives him a "No" gesture)

HANK (Cont'd)

What are "Flippins"?

MAGGIE

Flippins are cinnamon and sugar pancakes - made real thin. We serve 'em with warm sliced apples. People come in from the collar counties for our Flippins! Excuse us a minute.

(MAGGIE takes MOLLY aside)

MOLLY

What, Mags?

MAGGIE

How about I help you close up and we go to "The Last Call" for a beer?

MOLLY

Well, I don't know if it would cheer me up or make things worse. ..I suppose maybe after this guy goes.

MAGGIE

Wanna ask him to go with us?

MOLLY

Magpie! Were you cooking this up while I was changing my shoes?

MAGGIE

No, but he seems like an ok sort of guy...

MOLLY

I don't know, ... the grill is off.

(She looks back at HANK)

But, he's probably going to be leaving soon.

MAGGIE

Oh, come on - it won't hurt to ask. If you want, I'll ask him.

(MAGGIE doesn't wait for MOLLY to answer, turns and approaches HANK with MOLLY on her heels)

MAGGIE

Hank, ... Molly and I thought you might like to join us for a drink. How 'bout it?

HANK

Uh, I don't know....It sounds tempting, ... but it's been a long day for me.

(HANK rises to leave)

MOLLY

And you have quite a drive ahead of you. Wouldn't you like to get something in your stomach first? This watering hole isn't far and they serve food.

HANK

Well,... all I've had since lunch is coffee and some mints I found in the glove compartment, ... but, it's getting late. I should go.

MOLLY

Stupid me, I turned off the grill without thinking. Sorry, Hank. I could make you a sandwich for the road?

(HANK is now at the door, thermos in hand)

HANK

No, but thanks for letting me bend your ear.

MAGGIE

(Hoping to change his mind one last time)

What a shame, seein' how it's barbecue pork sandwich and quarter draft night!

(HANK stops in his tracks, turns around)

HANK

Now you've done it. I love barbecue pork sandwiches.

MAGGIE

So you're coming with us?

HANK

How far is this place?

MAGGIE

Oh, maybe 10 or 15 minutes away, depending upon which part of the fork we take.

HANK

Okay, you got me.

MAGGIE

Great! And I thought this evening would be a total wash. Molly - don't just stand there, go back upstairs and change, while I set up the coffee station for the breakfast crowd.

(MOLLY starts to exit left, then stops)

MOLLY

Oh! I almost forgot. What about Jake? He's going to throw a fit!

HANK

Just _how_ early are you closing?

MAGGIE

Oh,...by the time we lock up, maybe 45 minutes. Besides, Jake's gone. He took off right after I got here.

(with a coy smile, MAGGIE goes to coffee station behind counter)

MOLLY

He did? And he was so worried about customers.... I suppose I'd better change.

(MOLLY exits stage left, untying her apron)

HANK

Here's a few more.

(HANK brings misc. cups etc. to MAGGIE)

MAGGIE

You need me to rinse out that thermos?

HANK

Oh, no, it's fine. ...

(He sets thermos back at booth)

MAGGIE

That about does it. Excuse me while I go light a fire under Molly.

(She crosses with purse, towards stage left)

While you're waiting for us girls, why don't you play some music? Good luck in finding anything from the last few decades. Jake doesn't exactly keep it up to date.

(MAGGIE exits stage left, the "ghost" of RENEE, "seen" only by audience, enters past her and sits at counter. HANK at table. RENEE is dressed in worn jeans and a vintage Chicago Cubs jersey, playing with a baseball. HANK sets thermos down, removes cap and pulls a folded piece of paper from it)

40

RENEE

"I, Renee Frances Vinette, being of sound mind and body, this 13th day of June, 1993, do hereby request that my ashes be spread on Wrigley Field."... I Guess you're going to have to go with plan "A" and get some zip-lock bags tomorrow. I'll keep my fingers crossed that the wind will be blowing in. Fewer homers, of course, but, oh well.

HANK

What a mess this is! It sure doesn't seem like three and a half years ago since I found this in the safety deposit box. Should have shown it to Dad right away. THERE! I finally said it out loud! IT WAS ME!! I FOUND IT-NOT DAD!!

RENEE

Confession may be good for the soul, but it's useless keep going over this.

HANK

When I lied and told him that I just found this, he was so disappointed that he couldn't make the trip with me! That made me feel even worse!.... The lie just keeps getting bigger. I lied to Molly when she asked me why I waited so long. God! I'm such a coward – pretending that Dad was the procrastinator and not me!!

RENEE

You always did leave your homework 'til the last minute.

HANK

This is quite a haul to Chicago. I could have used Dad's company. Instead, I waited until it was impossible for him to come with me!

RENEE

Could have been like old times – the three of us at a ballgame! Anyway, this was supposed to be a road trip, not a guilt trip.

HANK

Since I started veterinary school, all I could think about was finishing as quickly as possible. Some social life! Book work and farm animals. How sick is that?....So, I lied to Dad, I'm sure Mom knows, some how,...Molly, Doc and Ebbets – that's five people.

RENEE

And to yourself,...that makes six.

HANK

And to myself, that's six!!

RENEE

I know you've been working hard and that you're lonely, Son, but you need to lighten up.

HANK

Today is the first day in a while that I don't smell like a pig sty or have cow dung in the treads of my shoes! ... Last night I dreamed that, as punishment for lying to Dad, he died <u>before</u> I got back from Chicago. What if that comes true? Then what?

RENEE

Then I tell him "mission accomplished" when he gets here... <u>I</u> never used guilt as a motivator. You must have gotten that from Dad's side of the family.

HANK

Mom, ...you always knew what to say.

RENEE

I'll see what I can do. In the mean time, quit your belly-aching and enjoy the rest of the evening. How often do you get stuck in the middle of two lovely girls?

HANK

I guess you just never know what the day's gonna bring.

(He crosses to juke box, scans title choices and turns back to booth)

HANK (Cont'd)

This one's for you, Mom.

(HANK puts coins in, presses buttons, plays "You Got It" by Roy Orbison. He stays at juke box, hovering over it to read the titles. RENEE can't resist keeping time to the music. She puts down the ball and gets up to dance)

RENEE

Good choice!

(HANK notices "Open" sign needs turning. He goes to the door and looks out to see if anyone's coming, then turns the sign over and returns to the table)

(Lights dim out)

ACT I, SCENE 2

(The following morning. There is a knock at the diner door which becomes increasingly louder)

(HANK calls out as he pounds harder on the door)

HANK

Molly! **HELLO! MOLLY!**

JAKE

Molly! For cryin' out loud - you got customers!

(MOLLY comes in from kitchen, turns lights on from behind counter, tries tying her apron as she approaches the door)

MOLLY

I'm comin', I'm comin'! Hold your horses.

(MOLLY unlocks the door and opens it. HANK enters, wrapped in a pink blanket with yellow and white flowers, and holding a sports bag)

HANK

Mornin'.

MOLLY

Good morning, Hank. How long have you been out there?

HANK

Not long....This must be your blanket. Thanks.

(HANK puts down bag, folds up blanket with MOLLY'S help and hands it over to her. HANK rubs his cramped shoulders and neck)

MOLLY

Did you get any sleep in your car?

HANK

Oh, yeah. It's amazing how a long day and one beer can knock a guy out.

MOLLY

I wasn't sure if Maggie talked you into a deep sleep or what.

HANK

Well, she was pretty talkative on the way over. But, as I recall, we no sooner ordered drinks and food and Maggie ditched us.

MOLLY

That's Maggie.... Well, the barbecue sandwiches were great, weren't they?

HANK

Oh yeah! The best barbecue pork I've tasted in a while. You're the only person I know who puts dill pickles on them, like I do.

MOLLY

I could make a meal out of just those pickles!

HANK

I'm sure I made a pig out of myself.... Once I started eating, I realized just how starved I was. But, besides the food,...I had a great time.

MOLLY

Me too. I can't remember the last time I drove a car. Jake has one, but he doesn't let me use it very often.

HANK

Thanks for driving back here. It's a good thing I didn't get back on the interstate last night. I just couldn't keep my eyes open any longer!

MOLLY

By the time I pulled into the parking lot, you were out cold. I didn't see any point in waking you up. I hope you were warm enough out there..

(HANK picks up his bag)

HANK

Thanks to the <u>lovely</u> blanket, I was just fine.

MOLLY

I was thinking,…there's a place called Dwyerstown or Byersville or somethin' on the other side of Dubuque. It's where that baseball movie "Field of Dreams" was filmed.

HANK

Oh, Dyersville. Sure, I've heard of it.

MOLLY

Well, couldn't you go there to spread your mom's ashes? It's got real grass, and I've heard it's kind of magical.

HANK

No, it just wouldn't be the same. It's Wrigley or bust,… but thanks for the thought.

(HANK notices MOLLY's apron is untied)

Molly?

MOLLY

Yes?

(HANK puts down his bag and approaches her)

HANK

Your apron, umm. Hold still.

(HANK carefully ties her apron and fixes her collar.

He lets a hand rest on her shoulder, which she touches)

MOLLY

Thanks.

HANK

Molly, do you,....

MOLLY

What?

HANK

Just wondering out loud.

MOLLY

About...?

HANK

About hind-sight and changing a screw up.

MOLLY

You mean, go back to the past and fix something? Sounds like time travel.

HANK

Yeah. If you could return to that crazy minute and stretch it out in slow motion. .

MOLLY

That'd be great! I'm sure most everybody would jump at the chance to change at least one really stupid thing they did, with me at the front of the line.

HANK

If I figure out a way to hit rewind, I'll let you know. I should get cleaned up.

MOLLY

I know you're frustrated with your trip, but do you have <u>any</u> idea how lucky you are?

HANK

Right now I don't feel so lucky.

MOLLY

No,... I mean that you're lucky to have had a close family. And how is it that you're so sure about <u>what</u> you want and <u>where</u> you want to go?

HANK

Not sure, just flexible. My mom's favorite saying was, "While you're out, anything's on the way!" Never mind that she didn't know how to drive. I do know I'm lucky.

(JAKE interrupts as he comes out to the counter from the kitchen)

JAKE

You still here! Molly, you didn't let this free-loader sleep in one of the booths, did you?

49

HANK

I slept in my car, ...so?

JAKE

So, you got money for breakfast, " Mr. Sports Bag"?

MOLLY

Jake!

HANK

I have money. I'll be back in a few minutes, Molly.

(HANK goes to men's room and MOLLY goes behind the counter, past JAKE, stroking the blanket as she goes to find a place for it)

JAKE

After the loser eats, he's outta here.

MOLLY

FINE! But I'll be surprised if he stays for coffee after you treated him so rudely!

JAKE

So what? Inside of an hour he'll be gone. You sure can pick 'em.

(JAKE exits to kitchen, as MAGGIE enters dressed to waitress)

MAGGIE

Hey, Molly!

MOLLY

Hey.

(MAGGIE puts purse behind counter)

MAGGIE

I saw Hank's car is still here. Where'd he go,... the little boy's room?

MOLLY

Uh, huh.

MAGGIE

Don't tell me he slept in his car!

MOLLY

Yeah.

(MAGGIE notices that MOLLY is having a hard time refilling a napkin holder at the counter)

MAGGIE

Good golly, Miss Molly! You're gonna cram that so full, it'll take a crow bar to get one out! What's wrong?

MOLLY

Nothing.

MAGGIE

Doesn't look like nothing.

(MAGGIE hugs her as JAKE comes out to pour himself a cup of coffee)

JAKE

The grill's on.

(sarcastically)

Sorry to interrupt this tender moment, but you forgot to flip over the "Open" sign.

(JAKE gets a cup of coffee and returns to the kitchen. MOLLY breaks away to turn over the sign on the door. As MOLLY exits to the kitchen, a regular customer comes in)

MAGGIE

Mornin' Cliff.

CLIFF

Mornin'.

(MAGGIE brings him coffee)

MAGGIE

What'll it be today?

CLIFF

A short stack of Flippins with a side of bacon and keep the coffee comin'.

MAGGIE

Rough night?

CLIFF

No, but I'm headed into Chi-Town. It's going to be a long day.

(MAGGIE goes into the kitchen to place the order, MOLLY comes back out)

MOLLY

Hey Cliff, how're you today?

CLIFF

Ok, how's it goin', Molly?

MOLLY

Fine ... I guess.

> (she realizes that CLIFF is staring at her, she stands up and straightens out of her slump and changes the subject)

Where to this mornin'?

> (CLIFF is in the middle of a gulp of coffee as MAGGIE comes out of the kitchen and answers for him)

MAGGIE

Cliff's headed for Chicago today, aren't ya, Cliff?

CLIFF

Yeah.

MOLLY

Chicago, huh. Why so far?

CLIFF

I'm haulin' a back-up order for Cubs Park. Our location closer to the city ran short,...with so many homes springin' up 'n all.

> (MOLLY has been listening politely, but is visibly distracted)

MOLLY

Oh,... I see....

CLIFF

Molly?.... Uh,... Molly? Could I get a warmer?

MOLLY

Uh,... sure. Sorry, Cliff. I must be day dreamin'....There ya go.

CLIFF

Thanks.

(MAGGIE returns to the kitchen. HANK comes out of the Men's Room with his sports bag. He has changed his shirt)

MOLLY

Where are you sittin' Hank?

HANK

The counter's fine.

(HANK sits at counter with one space between himself and CLIFF. MAGGIE comes out of the kitchen with CLIFF's order)

MAGGIE

Well, if it isn't Sleeping Beauty.

(She winks at Hank, then serves CLIFF)

HANK

Hi, Maggie.

MAGGIE

Hi, there.

(MAGGIE takes a tray with condiments, salt and pepper shakers, etc. to distribute to the eating areas)

MOLLY

Can I get you some breakfast, Hank?

HANK

You sure can,.... let's see, ... orange juice, coffee and um, ..

(He looks at what CLIFF has)

CLIFF

I highly recommend the Flippins!

MOLLY

Flippins comin' right up.

(MOLLY exits to kitchen)

CLIFF

Regulars get off the interstate just for these!

HANK

I see, ...What's the best way to get back onto the interstate?

CLIFF

Well, what ever you do, don't take either side of the fork, you'll just get lost.

Turn right out of the parking lot and follow it back to the gas station about two miles down. You'll see the exit signs there.

HANK

Okay, thanks.

(MOLLY brings HANK'S juice and coffee)

HANK

Thanks, Molly.... That reminds me, I should probably get gas before I go much further.

CLIFF

I'll be headin' out in a few, if you wanna follow me.

HANK

Thanks again, but I'm sure I can find it.

(MAGGIE comes back to counter with the tray and baseball)

MAGGIE

Hey, look what I found.

HANK

Let's see!

(HANK takes the ball from MAGGIE and looks it over carefully)

MOLLY

Is it yours? You were the last one to sit there yesterday.

MAGGIE

It's got some signature on it. Billy,…

HANK

Let's see. Billy Williams. It's a sign!… It's a, uh, sign that I, um, I'm getting spacey.…It's mine, all right. I guess I forgot to zip up my bag.

CLIFF

That's a real collectors item! You shouldn't be traipsin' around with it in your bag.

(HANK puts the ball in his sports bag and zips it up)

HANK

You're right.… I should be more careful.

MAGGIE

Need a warmer before you go, Cliff?

CLIFF

No, thanks. ... What are the damages?

(CLIFF leaves tip, rises to pay MAGGIE at the register, then crosses to use Men's Room. MAGGIE clears his place)

JAKE

ORDER!

(JAKE's voice shakes MOLLY out of her trance)

MOLLY

Oh! That's your breakfast, Hank.

(MOLLY goes into kitchen and returns immediately with a plate of flippins, then refills his coffee without asking)

HANK

Thanks.

(MOLLY returns to the kitchen)

MAGGIE

So Hank, what do you think of our "World Famous Flippins" ?

HANK

Delicious,... especially with these warm apples.

MAGGIE

Delicious enough to bring you back this way?

                              HANK

Most definitely!

                    (CLIFF enters from Men's Room and wave as MOLLY comes out
                    of the kitchen)

                              CLIFF

See ya, Mags, Molly.

                              MAGGIE

Bye, Cliff.

                              MOLLY

Have a safe trip.

                    (the girls give a little wave and CLIFF exits)

                    (MAGGIE starts making it up as she goes, looking for an excuse
                    to leave HANK and MOLLY alone)

                              MAGGIE

Well,...um, Jake wants the fridge cleaned out today when it's slow.

.... uh, so call me if it gets busy, okay?

                    (MAGGIE exits to kitchen while HANK finishes his breakfast)

                              MOLLY

Isn't that a coincidence - Cliff's heading to Chicago today, too.

                              HANK

He is? Did he mention where in Chicago?

MOLLY

Something about bears,... or cubs in a park.... I don't know, maybe a zoo?

HANK

Bears, ... cubs, ... cubs,... park? He's going to Cubs Park?

MOLLY

Yeah, that sounds like what he said. More coffee?

HANK

It sure is a coincidence. Cubs Park and Wrigley Field are the same place.

MOLLY

They are?....

(She stops, looks at the door, then at HANK and starts jumping up and down)

Oh my God! Hank! Where is your thermos?

HANK

It's in the car,...why?

MOLLY

Go get it!

HANK

Why?

MOLLY

Quick! You've got to stop Cliff!

HANK

Calm down, Molly! Why?

MOLLY

Cliff drives a <u>sod</u> truck! That's what he's taking into Chicago! Don't you see -

You could put the thermos, I mean the ashes on the sod! Hurry!

(HANK finally realizes what she's saying and bolts through the door. MOLLY runs to look out the window. She paces back and forth, then looks back out the window, then paces some more. She goes to the counter and clears the dishes, then nervously starts wiping down the counter and booths while waiting. All the time muttering.)

MOLLY

Come on, Hank..... .

(lights out as spot comes up on HANK and CLIFF downstage left)

HANK

Now you're sure, Cliff?

CLIFF

Well, it's the strangest thing I've ever heard of,....but it makes pretty darn good sense....Yeah, I'm sure. Only, you do understand that I'm just droppin' the load off, right?

HANK

Right. That's fine. Short of hiring a helicopter, this is my last, best chance to do this.

CLIFF

Are you headin' to this afternoon's game? 'Cause if y'are, the sod won't be put down 'til after the game's over. It's a good thing they watered it down.

HANK

I was so excited, I didn't even think about that.

CLIFF

Yeah, the Cubs' next road trip is so short that the groundskeepers will have to hustle.

HANK

That's okay,.... I'll take my chances.

CLIFF

Come with me, and I'll show ya what section to spread those, uh,... ashes on.

HANK

I hate holding up your trip like this, Cliff, but I really need a moment.

CLIFF

I better leave ya to it then. I'll go undo part of the tarp and unroll a piece of sod for ya. Just come around to the front of the truck when you're ready.

(CLIFF exits stage right)

(HANK looks at thermos and begins)

HANK

Remember when Dad would drive us to the nearest baseball diamond as soon as the ground was dry enough? We'd all jump out of the car and race to home plate. The first one that tagged it and yelled " PLAY BALL" got to bat.... It took me a while to catch on that you were giving me a head start.

(HANK starts crossing right to where light comes up on "sod bundles" with the "ghost" of RENEE standing nearby)

61

HANK (Contd.)

Well, looks like I'm getting a head start too.

RENEE

Don't be late for the game, Hank. You know the rule is that you have to be in your seat <u>before</u> the National Anthem starts.

HANK

When the umpire shouts, "PLAY BALL!", I'll hear your voice. And when the food and drink vendors bark and chant, I'll hear you mimicking them quietly. By the way, I don't know how you managed the baseball, but thanks.

RENEE

You're welcome, Son. I love you.

HANK

You'll have a bumpy ride today, but somehow, I think you must have planned it.

(HANK starts slowly humming "Take Me Out to the Ballgame" while he uncaps the thermos and carefully distributes ashes on sod)

RENEE

Thanks for everything.

(RENEE quietly joins in the song, then disappears into the darkness at the end. HANK exits stage right)

(Stage lights up as MOLLY is still pacing and cleaning nervously. She takes one more look out a window then backs off towards the counter)

MOLLY

There goes Cliff. Hank must have stopped him before he drove off. I wonder what.....

(MAGGIE interrupts MOLLY's train of thought as she comes out of the kitchen)

MAGGIE

Molly,...did Hank take off already?

(MOLLY and MAGGIE watch as HANK comes back in. He has a distant look on his face as he stares at the empty thermos.)

MOLLY

Hank?

HANK

Molly!

(HANK sets down thermos, picks MOLLY up, spins her around and plants a kiss on her lips)

Molly the Wonder Woman! THANK YOU!....THANK YOU!.... THANK YOU!

MAGGIE

What'd I miss?

(MOLLY is smiling, but embarrassed by the attention)

MOLLY

You caught Cliff! I'm so glad!

HANK

Just in time, too...How can I ever,...I mean,...Molly, you've saved the day!!!

MAGGIE

Molly?

MOLLY

Oh, Mags, it's nothing .... tell you later.

HANK

Well - now you <u>have</u> to come with me!

MOLLY

Where?

HANK

To the game! The baseball game!

MAGGIE

The baseball game?

MOLLY

Oh, Hank,...I don't know.... All the way to Chicago?

MAGGIE

CHICAGO?

HANK

Come on! Please?

MOLLY

I mean, it sounds exciting, and I've never seen Chicago either. Are you sure?

HANK

Of course I'm sure. You just <u>have</u> to come with me! I feel like celebrating and I can't think of anyone I'd rather spend the day with!

MAGGIE

Go ahead Molly!

MOLLY

I'd really love to go, but what about Jake?

MAGGIE

Oh, for heaven's sake, Molly! What about Jake? You go ahead. I'll handle Jake.

MOLLY

But, you'll be stuck here all day.

MAGGIE

So, what? You've covered for me plenty of times.

HANK

Come on, Molly. We'll have some time before the game to sight-see... please?

(MOLLY looks at both of them with a wild smile)

MOLLY

Okay!

HANK

Great! You won't regret it!

(He turns MOLLY around, unties her apron)

You'll need a jacket, it gets chilly downtown.

(MOLLY takes off apron and exits quickly stage left)

MAGGIE

Well, Hank....I'm not quite sure what you're celebrating.... And, I can't remember the last time she took a day off in the middle of the week. But, this is great! It's just what Doctor Maggie ordered. Thank you!

(MOLLY enters from stage left with Dean's old leather jacket)

MOLLY

I'm ready!

HANK

You have time to change, if you want.

MOLLY

No, I just want to get going before Jake finds out.

(JAKE comes out from kitchen)

JAKE

Before Jake finds out what? Where in the HELL do you think you're goin'?

(MOLLY is speechless)

HANK

Molly and I are going to Chicago for the day.

JAKE

I ain't talkin' to you, jerk-bag! I'm talkin' to Molly. So, Molly, you're just gonna run off like a tramp with some stranger?

HANK

Look, she can make up her own mind…

(MOLLY cuts HANK off)

MOLLY

How dare you call me a tramp, Jake!

JAKE

Well, you're actin' just like one !

MOLLY

Going into Chicago for the day doesn't make me a tramp. I'm over 21 and don't need your permission! And besides,… Hank's no stranger. I feel like I know him better in the few hours that I've talked to him, than, well, even YOU!

JAKE

Listen up, you half-wit. If you leave me short-handed, you can just look for somewhere else to work!

MOLLY

Oh, yeah,…well,… maybe I'll find a place where I don't have to deal with some old crab that complains from morning 'til night!

(surprised at her own outburst, MOLLY covers her mouth)

JAKE

That's right, just dig yourself in deeper.

HANK

Come on, Molly. Everything will be fine.

(MAGGIE takes JAKE aside)

MAGGIE

I can solo this without Molly for once, Jake.

JAKE

Thanks, Maggie! You're a big help! For all we know, " Mr. Nice Guy"
here is some psycho who's driving around with a dead body in the trunk
of his car!

MAGGIE

Jake, you watch way too much T.V.... Your sister isn't stupid....If she trusts
Hank, that's good enough for me.

JAKE

Yeah,... well,... she trusted Tony, too, and look what happened with him.

MAGGIE

Hank is different. I had time to talk to him yesterday and take it from me,
he's no psycho.

JAKE

I'll bet Molly doesn't even know his last name.

MAGGIE

Why don't you ask her?

JAKE

Okay, I will.

(turns to MOLLY)

Molly, I'll bet you a day off that you don't know this guy's last name **OR** anything about him!

MOLLY

Hank's studying to be a veterinarian, he's from Iowa and his last name is Aaron. HA!

JAKE

(to MAGGIE)

See what I mean? Hank Aaron, is it? Right! And I'm Jackie Robinson!

MAGGIE

She's right, Jake, that's his real name.

HANK

Don't even think about asking me to see an I.D.

JAKE

You two'd stick together just to prove me wrong!

MOLLY

Right or wrong, I'm still taking the day!

(MAGGIE takes blanket from behind counter for MOLLY)

MAGGIE

Go ahead, you two.... Here, you might need this.

JAKE

Great! I gotta put up with Maggie-the-mouth all day!

MAGGIE

I swear to God, Jake! One more word and you can run this place all by yourself.

JAKE

Don't threaten me, Maggie. I could replace your smartass attitude in a minute!

(to HANK and MOLLY with resolve)

Go on, get out of here.

(JAKE exits)

MAGGIE

Now hit the road. Have a hot dog and beer for me!

MOLLY

But, Mags,...I....

MAGGIE

Don't worry, Molly. The big jerk will cool off eventually.

MOLLY

Maybe.

(HANK picks up sports bag)

MOLLY (Cont'd)

How 'bout that blanket, Magpie?

(MAGGIE gives the blanket to MOLLY)

MOLLY (Cont'd)

Thanks, I owe you one.... Wait!

(MOLLY gives jacket to MAGGIE)

MAGGIE

Molly, ... are you sure?

HANK

You should definitely take the jacket, Molly. Chicago weather is really fickle.

(MOLLY takes back jacket)

HANK

Thanks, Maggie. And, just for the record, my last name is Vinette.

MAGGIE

Okay, Mr. Hank Aaron Vinette, I just have one request.

HANK

Anything! You want us to bring you back a souvenir?

MAGGIE

No. No souvenirs. I just want <u>you</u> to let me in on your little secret.

(HANK and MOLLY look at each other)

HANK

It's well,...complicated and, umm,... It 'll have to keep 'til we get back.

MAGGIE

Fine, now scram you two!

                    HANK
See ya!

                    MOLLY
Bye!

        (JAKE enters from kitchen)

                    JAKE
Maggie, you got a fridge to clean.

        {Jake looks at MOLLY and HANK, takes a deep breath)

Have a good time.

                    MAGGIE
That was a real decent thing you just did.

        (kisses JAKE on the cheek)

Who knew?

        (MAGGIE exits into kitchen)

        (JAKE exits into kitchen)

                    HANK
You're gonna love Chicago, Molly.

                    MOLLY
Are you sure we'll have enough time to sight-see before the game?

HANK

Yup, as long as we're in our seats when they play the National Anthem. That's the rule! By the way, you have unfair advantage.

MOLLY

I do?

HANK

Yes,… you know my full name, what's yours?

MOLLY

Molly Banks.

HANK

Banks?! Really? What's your middle name?

MOLLY

Oh, don't make me tell. It's so old fashioned and silly.

HANK

What if I guess it?

MOLLY

You can try but,…

HANK

Erin,…Erna, no,…Ernest,…umm,…is it Ernestine?

MOLLY

(in disbelief)

How did you,? Maggie doesn't even know it!

73

HANK

So, your full name is Molly Ernestine Banks.

MOLLY

Yes, why are you looking at me like that? I know it's different but,…

HANK

No Molly, it's,…it's perfect!

MOLLY

Something tells me this has to do with baseball.

HANK

I'll show you later.

(HANK and MOLLY exit. MAGGIE has put DEAN'S jacket on hook and notices HANK's thermos at the booth and crosses to pick it up)

MAGGIE

Would ya look at this filthy thing! Hank must have dropped it in the parking lot.

(she shakes her head in disgust and starts to wipe off the thermos)

And here I thought I was gonna have to watch Molly mope around 'til closing time.

(Reprise "You Got It", by Roy Orbison. MAGGIE exits. DEAN enters with a bag of peanuts and RENEE enters with open box of Cracker Jack. Both smile and exit. Lights fade out)

THE END

Printed in the United States
by Baker & Taylor Publisher Services

Printed in the United States
by Baker & Taylor Publisher Services